Afro Clouds & Nappy Rain

Afro Clouds & Nappy Rain

The Curtis Brown Poems

Poems by
James B. Golden

iUniverse, Inc.
Bloomington

Afro Clouds & Nappy Rain
The Curtis Brown Poems

iUniverse books may be ordered through booksellers or by contacting:

iUniverse
1663 Liberty Drive
Bloomington, IN 47403
www.iuniverse.com
1-800-Authors (1-800-288-4677)

ISBN: 978-1-4620-5512-8 (sc)
ISBN: 978-1-4620-5513-5 (hc)
ISBN: 978-1-4620-5514-2 (ebk)

Printed in the United States of America

iUniverse rev. date: 10/07/2011

To all of my boys, but especially Jared, Micheal, Kevin, Angel, Darnell & Everett, La Troy, Chris, Joseph and Little Paul—

This collection is for every misunderstood

Curtis Brown in the world . . .

Let the rain kiss you. Let the rain beat upon your head with silver liquid drops. Let the rain sing you a lullaby.

—Langston Hughes

And it shall come to pass, when I bring a cloud over the earth, that the bow shall be seen in the cloud . . .

—Genesis 9:14

Contents

Nappy Rain

Purple Sun

Preface

Curtis Brown is a character who represents many young Black and Brown men raised within a society which has deemed them dangerous and intellectually inferior. He is the sum of several boys and men I've known richly over the years, including me. These poems are wildly exciting, peaceful, frightening, at times blatantly explicit, and unabashedly honest.

The explicit language in many of the poems is absolutely necessary to convey the rawness of depression. I've often thought of universal expression, but I will not *pop for you or break for you*, especially in my writing.

I challenge the reader to experience the vast emotional nightmare of a child abandoned by his prostitute mother, molested by a family member and trapped in a debilitating depression.

In "Why Black Men Must Go To Therapy", I wrote similarly about the mental state of many boys like Curtis.

In reality, our blues are simply untreated diagnoses which have caused us to self-medicate with drugs and alcohol. We walk around daily with full-sized depression, anxiety, anger, schizophrenia and bi-polar disorder. We live in bubbles and tread lightly around our friends and family, yet cry in dark spaces, praying that the voices and thoughts will be eradicated from our minds. (Golden, James B. Clutch Magazine. August 2011)

Though the book is largely centered around the title character, many of the poems in *Afro Clouds & Nappy Rain* have been entwined with personal narrative and understandings. The series of tribute poems are people who have wildly affected me throughout my life.

As for Curtis, he is a living being who wrestles with the powerlessness and hopelessness of his generation. By the end of the book, he finally decides whether or not to end his young life.

I hope that this book will inspire readers to look beyond the rough exterior of young troubled males, and find the golden spirits that exist behind the masks.

With a bit more understanding and empathy for their experiences, they are destined to see the brilliance of a fresh day.

The purple sun will emerge from behind the afro clouds and the nappy rain will go far, far away—revealing a handsome bow.

James B. Golden
September, 2011

Afro Clouds

Beautiful

Beautiful, Beautiful Black Boy,
eyes dark as
midnight.

Love the skin you're in,
rub lotion on it every
chance you get.

Breath into those
big brown nostrils
the air of a new hope.

Kiss the mirror frequently
and smile with your
eyes the size of
watermelon slices.

Beautiful, Beautiful Black Boy,
dance around the room
and land on your back
with arms and legs
praising God, facing
heaven, then wipe
the sweat off your
forehead and collect your
shadow

Seashores Look Down On Me

Dropped off of hanging stars
from a black empty space
vortex to underwater
lava-filled earth centers.
Low enough to smell the stench of hell.

So low
       low in the waters,
seashores look down on me.

And massage my collars
making paper planes of my
tattered Prince t-shirt
quietly robbing my lowered
heart-strings planting
forests in my nucleus.

Low
       low enough to swim
amongst the flames.

Rotten Diamonds On The Inside

Got rotten diamonds on
the inside
molded apples in my
core.

Puffed up like
corn kernels frying
deep in Crisco-greased
skillets.

Suckered into untimely
tear drops plunging in
to a rushing slowing
bloodstream.

Encased by pit bulls
gnawing at my neck,
leeches gasping for
skin scales.

Chocolate-covered diamonds
rotten on the inside.

Don't Touch My Hair

Power powdered chocolate
sliced slats dripping down my
back like spikes on a porcupine's
tail.

And this woman just
placed her hand in a trap
laced with 3,000
mini-mite strand pricklies.

Cause I don't allow no one to
touch my hair.

It's like brushing a hand against
broken barbed upright fences
a shocking series of slicing
thorny rose bush stems
uprooted in a summer's
2:00 PM.

Ma'am, please don't
harass my consciousness.

Don't assault the reincarnation of
Bob Marley's crown atop my head.

Do us all a favor and stare—
but leave my humanity in its
nappy Black highchair,
and don't you dare touch my hair.

I Rise Up In You

I rise up in you
like yesterday when
feet went smashing down
to drum beats in the
West African midnight

stomping out demons
from baby boys your age.

I rise up in you
on those days we
sat in "white-only"
restaurants guarding our stomachs,
not eating a morsel
not batting an eyelid
never saying a mumbling word—
til you let me eat
with no consequence of
separatist backlash.

I rise up in you
on Sunday mornings
dressed in
linen suits, fedoras,
handkerchiefs. Humming a
"Welllllllll" or
"How I got over—been a
long long journey, my soul
looks back in wonder . . . how I
got over"

over crack cocaine in the 80s
when I rose up in you.
Distributed largely in urban
Black/Brown slums, shot up
and snorted into brain matter
waiting to discover the cure for
AIDS. Needles dancing around
his arm, Michael moonwalking
down a back alley.

And still I rise up in you
especially when Black men are
beaten by police officers—chastised
like dogs defecating on living room
carpets. Michael Vick fighting bulls.
Robert Kelly pissing on girls
after school.

I rise up in you
like Sean Bell rose to heaven
after 50 gunshot booms in
his chest and stomach,
'fraid of NYPD's historical
tendencies to shoot first.

FEMA's natural tendency to
let human beings get sucked
underneath 75,000 pounds of
New Orleans swamp water
neglecting a weakening levee.

I rise up in you
like Tupac Shakur did all
those immortalized "Thug Life"
lies and hypermasculine
confused graffiti etched
on his stomach. Spitting lines
back and forth between

Brenda and *Hit Em Up*.
Changes—can't a brotha
get a little peace?

So I can rise up in you
like Jordan tennis shoes
eroding your mother's pocketbook
for a $150.00 pair of rubber mass,
tacky cheaply-made
stompers—sewn together
in 118° sweatshops filled
with 525 Chinese 10-year-olds
paid $0.50 per hour
molested by Nike's over-zealous
need to create buyers who can't
afford their solid
Dunks.

I rise up in you
like soul food on Sunday afternoon
at 3:00 PM. Buttered cornbread,
fried chicken, a little candied yams,
pork chops, collard greens, coleslaw,
gumbo and rice, chicken and dumplings,
green beans with sliced potatoes,
banana pudding, peach cobbler,
sweet potato pie baked beneath the sun's broiler,
hamhocks smothered in the
cholesterol-flavored gravy, macaroni and
cheese baked in high blood pressure's
oven.

Even then, I rise up in you
like sports and dance—
the only things we do well
right?

Mis-educated on the discovery of sciences and
formulation of astrology and
open-heart surgeries and freedom
political strategies, we drew
the original hieroglyphics,
used the power of the
drum beat to communicate
before formal speech,
we created the stoplight,
hotcomb, peanut butter, IBM,
jazz, blues, gospel, rap, R&B
like Whitney singing "my love is
your love"/ Bob wailing
"emancipate yourself from mental slavery"/
Fiasco motivating us to "kick, push"/
Badu's soapy sad love songs.

I rise up in Cube's "today was a good day"
          Big's "it was all a dream"
          Mary's "you remind me"

Set in a scene above all the
times I couldn't swim in your
pools or walk through
hotel lobbies.

I rise up in Barack Obama
standing tirelessly through
forecasted storms pelting
him with the hail of un-democracy.
Unyielding to holding King's dream
in his sweaty palms

dripping jheri curl juice in
the White House.

Catfish and red snapper
kitchen scents driving out to
greet us on those West African mornings
laying Kente cloth on the
dining room table.

Planting seeds in your
brown-baby-boy
brain matter. Rising up
like a loaf of bread
filled with yeast.

In this classroom—
in my seat.

Begging you to claim your
un-defeat

standing up with unshakeable
cultural pride

tears tumbling from the corners
of your eyes

singing the words as I
rise up in you—in 1952
like yesterday's dawn

facing the rising sun
of our new day begun
let us march on
til' victory
is
won

Afro Clouds

I've always loved in the
strangest places
and remained in strained
relations,
just to be close to your
love.

Jumped rivers in rush hour
fought bees for the flowers
sat on nappy textured power
just to be close to your
love.

April came and left by May
Spring goes up and drifts away
you were always there
consistent in my dreams
especially on that
fateful evening.

Took my soul on up above the clouds,
rainbows, rose petals, float like doves
steal me back
close to your
love.

Brother, Brother

since you left,
life's been a mess
met with yellow tender trees
and a baby on my knees

stop crying, son—
stop crying
a free belief in the brief

brother, brother
take that backward hat off me
jeans sagging lowly
showing my boxer briefs

out like a homo on the yard
gawking at the movie star
swangin' that thang around
the many faces of the many men
who've attacked his many manhoods

like daggers
      daggers
           daggers
                daggers

James B. Golden

STABING—

brother, brother
take my grave up to the sky
floating on sapphire pools
face down—sucking air
from flying fishes and
the lips of drowned
babies—

flushed from the toilet
of our generation

Our Nig

a nigger is still a nigger
is still a nigger is still a
nigger.

and who are you?

a nigger

like a reproduced field hand
straddling massa's whip

like a body swinging
from a thorny noose
underneath the green and white
"a negro was lynched today"
sign atop the First Baptist Church
bell tower.

like a nigger-boy prying open
the swallowing alligator's
jaw.

a nigga

like Jay
pimpin all over
the world?
pimpin us all
the word.

Nothing But The Blues
(for Langston)

I don't want no half-steppin,
gyratin, vibrato-driven
gaping songs on my iPod.

No tappin, steppin, hip-raisin,
fetchet style gospel
bumping from my speakers.

I don't want my car blasting pitch-
perfect, foot-drummin, guitar strummin,
country swingers.

No hip, hip, hip battles beating
chests, flowing lyrics, bottle-
inducing, spirit-stabbing rap records.

No days filled with pure tonalities

Latin swingin,
African beatin,
J-hopin,
Beboppin,
indecipherous delicatessens,

I just want my blues.
Nothing but the blues.

The Hip Hop Suite:

I Am The Authentic Man
(Rap Version)

If God is a DJ, life is a dancefloor

—Pink

Churnin out beats twisted
like Kanye's brain pinwheeling
downward toward a
souled-out catalog

drumming up satisfactory
sounds, tumultuously turning
Timbaland toward towering
talents

spinning the nicest dusties
round and round like
Mary J, ringin around the
rosie

pockets full of hash
strolling down the walk
captured by the band,

I am the authentic man.

Slowly serenading the people
with revolutionary verbiage
vibrating across broken skins

kneeling,
head bowed and
body bent

throwing my hands up in the air
waving them 'round like I just don't care,
watching me "yooooooou" across the stage
making the jams rain
saving lives like I did
last night.

Over and over and over
and over 36 Chambers
with the Clan,
I am the authentic man.

He's the rapper
I'm the DJ,
spinning hot enough to
melt your face.

See, my albums bleed as if their sleeves speak,
the essence of my entire philosophy—
no one's greater than me

when it comes to setting up,
flippin' switches
hits and misses
a mic check
1-2   1-2,
shout out to
the honey out there
in her boo-coupe.

When I get to the stand
start scratchin' fingernails on hands
making dusties clap like no one can
spin those beats like it was planned
an original element oh so grand

I amaze my damn self and
fever burns my head
sweat protrudes from my glands

flip the switch to blow this mutha—
down with my mini fan,

I am the authentic man.

Didn't Ask You To Alter My Thoughts (On Vinyl)

it is never your fault
that I am this way.
just your fault that
I'm this pained.

you didn't create my
unhappy happenings,
only my reluctance to
pitter patter words together.

i didn't ask you to
alter my thoughts like
melded pennies   flattened
to jewelry.

just to be here.

can't love you anymore
for fear of losing you
for fear of losing you
for fear of losing you
for fear of losing you
for fear of losing you
for fear of losing you
for fear of losing you
for fear of losing you
for fear of losing you
for fear of losing you
for fear of losing you
for fear of losing you

for fear of loving you.
(((sorry—the track skipped)))

An Ode To Condoms

Dick
Dick
Hold your dick

Loaded weapons of mass
impregnating destruction,
pregnant Black gem
popping bubble gum riding
the A train
sportin gold hoops
swingin her head to
the bop bop   be be doo bop
of Beyonce's tune,
calling your genie closer
touching on the box like
a cheetah in heat
seducing the antelope nearer
to her huntress
meat

Hold your dick

Like it's running away from
your consciousness,
taking you on a ride
                    down
                             some
abandoned alley toward a
shadowy lamplight,
illuminating the WARNING sign
outside her bedroom gates

Stop it! Stop it!

Turn around and
hold your dick.

Curtis Brown

The Night You Had Sex With My Journal

Forget the night you slept with
my thoughts looming gracefully
round your eyeballs

fucking my words,
cumming on my pages.
notebooks scattered along
every constricted highway
saying goodbye Curtis—
see you in hell.

Robbing my soil's fertilizer
leaving my tree dying for
substance to make it grow again,
cleaning brain cavities and
clearing simple monstrosities from
my memories and youthful days,

sticking your penis
where it didn't belong
devirginizing my word womb
exposing all of
my insides.

You Gave Me April Rains In September

I woke up in color this morning
shined my shoes with a sun ray
brushed my teeth with a grapefruit
scrubbed my body with your hands.

The dew made me smile
as it sat on my skin
fresh winds blew from
my hair follicles to ends.

You gave me April rains
in September
and took away my
autumn skies.

Flowers dance
listlessly around
a purple sun and
unicorn-filled
clouds.

In The Presence Of Mine Enemies

Trembling,
balled up in a corner,
arms hugging knees,
juddering my body to keep warm,
darkness covers the room
emptiness lingers in its shadow.

Hear the creaks in the wood
above me,
in the presence of mine
enemies.

Pictures flash through my head
of a big black belly
hand cuffs,
dirty mattress,
hard dick, and there was
blood, blood, blood
dripping down to my
toes,
carving holes in my
soul, rearranging my
anxiety, taking the fight
out of me, pulling at
my core, steps get closer,
a light cracks in the room some more

In the presence of mine
enemies,
an open door

I gotta get off this floor.

You Raided My Flowing Ocean And Stole My Gold

Somewhere between yesterday
and the day before,

I was born

slicing my umbilical cord
of trampoline playing
in the summertime.

Earrings missing from
the lockbox of preciousness
and plummeting sorrow

like autumn succumbing to
Winter's dismal green-leaf-murdering
demands.

You raided my flowing ocean
and stole my gold

after I sang that song

gave you my last breath

and forgot to regret

you drained me

Letter No. 5 To An Absent Mother

Where are you Mommy?
I'm sorry.

*While I sit staring at
an unused apron perched up over
Nanny's kitchen sink*

Where is the 16 years of
unconditional maternal
conditioning you were supposed to
give me?

I walk around this empty
abode wondering how quickly
you walk daily to the
pusherman.

Pushing up explosives in your veins
like hospital needles
and morphine drips.

I'm in trouble because of you.
My heart keeps falling for
aged women, only to
crush underneath 40 pound
anxiety boulders.

Yesterday I thought I
saw you—as I drove
past Sepulveda Blvd.
rummaging through a catalogue
of prostitutes—

James B. Golden

Working hard for the money,
are you?

I sure am—working my
mind strings trying to comprehend
which of my actions caused
you to leave me.

Was it the time I peed in
the bed sheets after your
pimp bought me
some lonesome Christmas ago?

Perhaps it was on that
frozen February 21st in 1992
when I defied your wishes
birthing myself.

Days and days I've wished I could travel
back to that night when
I was conceived and beg your
trick to pop a condom.

Then it may have been somewhat
easier, existing in the
nothing.

Mommy, you missed the
rest of my growing's-up,
the questions I had about
my father—how to
keep my dick clean—the best way to get over a cold
in the wintertime.

You missed my first grade
spelling bee championship.
I didn't win, but I knew
how to spell S-Q-U-I-R-T.
It didn't matter
with you not there.

Like the pillowcases drenched
in tears everyday after
hearing "yo mama" jokes on the
school-yard during recess.

I knew they were all
true.

Sometimes I go out by myself
and paint pictures
where you win best actress
and I snag best supporting actor
in a film titled
Mother To Son—where you
gave me advice on what color
tie to wear to my 8th grade
graduation.

You would sing the main theme
like Whitney in
The Bodyguard.
I've pretended for years that's
your favorite movie.

I will always love you,
too—

would be stuck in the crevices
of my brain matter.

Then I would awake to
a musty air, surrounded by
my best friends anger and
resentment

sheets still stenched
from those days I found it hard
to get out of bed—

wishing I could smash into your
bedroom and tackle you
under covers on
Saturday mornings.

Today is your birthday, Mommy

but the darkness covers me instead.

Needless to say I miss you
and this is the finale to
your memory.

Fuck you, Mommy.
I'm sorry.

And This Is Not A Love Poem

I'm sorry,
I need you.
Like mountains rising through the
snow for God's kiss.

Apples rapidly covering cores
with flesh, skin, redness
crying out for the sensational
plucking from trees.

Dandelions brightening petals
elucidated like popcorn
kernels hatching.

I need you.
Like summer showers sitting
atop Georgia buildings
penetrating surfaces for
the cool breezes.

Bed sheets turning down,
frog legs high in mid-air traffic,
cell phones chirping for notice,
keys hanging lower and lower,

yesterday turning tomorrows,
midnights making daylight
saving deserted souls.

I need you.
Like sail boats and compasses.

Your Love Died In Me

Your love died in me
and laid buried in the
sand.

I tried to love you
and you left—

those thorny roses you gave me
sliced my cheeks like bread.

Every moment since then
your love died in me.

No room for
apathy, slowly slowing
my snowy insides.

Hollow baseball bats
crashing into my heart,
splintering my walls—

I belong to you
like sedated trees

Your love died in me.

Good Man

I'm a good man
but I've got troubled whims

stuck among the sea creatures
and purple tree leaves

yellow hued eyes
full watermelon lips
black heart

left in the oven on
360 degrees
180 minutes too long
like Thanksgiving ham bones
un-basted baking

yesterday my face fell off
presenting showing two gumdrop tinted
shades welled-up with
a reservoir of shower water

waiting on a phone call

from

you.

I Knew You Didn't Love Me

Your smile told me so
looking like grease-covered
paintings propped on
empty window seals.

Dropping tears into everlasting
buckets of lemon juice
suckled from the necks of
the wicked and impure.

Sailing on a sea of
self-hate, looking at
my body broken down like
bed sheets at 7:00 PM.
Bruised like rotting bananas
and spoiled green beans.

Gazing into a decomposing
face—watching doves
flounder away listlessly
in those eyes. Trying to
escape the victimizer cycle,
running round and round
like pinwheels stuck in
a whirlwind

and I knew you didn't love me.

Wings

I lost my wings
around 13
and never learned
to fly.

Jumped off the
ground but
tip-toes landed
back.

Only 5

Nice to meet you.

You finally came out to California.

Look how big the kids are.

This is sure to be our best Christmas yet.

Yes, he is five now—see how grown
he is?

*

Hi Denise—
Hi Curtis,
meet me tonight so I can
show you something.

*

Heart pacing like tramps galloping
through hallways.

Confused by
broken
puzzle pieces
flooding
my
mind matter.

Her.
Hand.
On.
My.
Dick.

Stroking up and down.

I was only 5.

Tasting her mountain peaks—
still growing into
womanhood,

smashing her pubescent
pussy against my shivering
body.

So cold, so cold.

Kissed me like goodbye
and silently gestured
us to secrecy.

*

Fucked my life
up.

Assassinated my manhood.

Stole my possibilities.

James B. Golden

*

Where were you?
I needed you to protect me—
I called and you didn't
come.

I was only 5.

Nappy Rain

Broken Pencils After Me

broken pencils after me
yellow swords,
my grief

lost my child
on an old dirt road

lost my heart
growing old

broken pencils after me
burning my tongue
like sunday morning
tea

just my mind
just my soul

on an old dirt road
on an old dirt road

Who Said You Could Have My Tears?

Borrow some,
but not all of my glass buckets
saturating this cotton marmalade-colored
t-shirt

On my smoothed-over
razor-close chocolate skin.

Panting, panting, pushing
none fell—constrained
detained in your unyielding
hand shake.

Let my tears go—
when down in Egypt land

Let my tears go—
like butter melts on non-stick pans

Let my tears go—
like my father on a sunny day

Let my tears go.

Seasons Always Change On Me

Scorching winters springing new
leaves on the cusp of freshly
birthed April midnights.

Turning showers of summer afternoons
into fall climates—
sycamores dropping leaves on
our sidewalk.

Turned into the glaring mask
of a purple sun—shining
up on beaches filled with
little bodies and flip flop
sandwiches.

32° snowflakes resting upon
the tip of a power pole
approaching the end of a
worn-down year.

Gaping for everlasting
security.

The Hunt

Crawling and running with
thoughts of golden
rainbows and spring
fires blazing up hills
made of milk chocolate
candies.

Stampeding atop lionesses
galloping through sub-Saharan
temperatures. Gazelles
dancing on their backs
legs reaching up
to the clouds.

Crawling and dancing with
wolves at my side
growling hyenas
racing to my
rotting corpse

blood crawling to
the cement.

The Vegan Poem

animal flesh
how I love my animal
flesh-drippings soaked
in lard and blood
swimming in plastic bacteria pools
lunching with
Styrofoam packaging and
unsanitary thermometers

cry little lamb as I grate your loins
let that fat sliver down my grill,
right through to my intestinal
walls.

The Sky's For Everyone

The sea's for nothing
sky's for everyone.
Staring, stirring earthen
coffee pots just to
smell the burning
flesh of a charred bean.

And so it is,
like you said it would be
close enough to kiss on the
lips, winking at the
whipped cloud shapes
on your cheek

dusting off the winds with
Windex

painting the sun purple
living in the sky
dying by the sea.

Holes In My Stomach

Open infected wounds
crying puss down my
love handles

stabbed into existence
by white-male-patriarchal
philosophies

redesigning and rearranging
my core,

displacing my thoughts
dismembering
my soul.

America Is Not My Home

You were hoping to take my
common sense away

and I knew you would.
Sensing a sensory time abuse
thrown in the faces of the poor

trying to convince me
—isms have ended since the
oppressor donned a black face.

I knew you would
and you did
take any
common sense away

replacing it with American
dreams and overpriced facial creams
telling me to concentrate
this camp is my home.

THIS CAMP IS NOT MY HOME

no home no home
this camp is not my home

not my home not my home
now my senses are all alone.

Crucify Me

I wake alone most mornings
to whistling winds roaring
bluebirds swimming outside
my bedroom window.

Some unholy evenings
spent lamenting God—
playing with his
resourcefulness—challenging.

All alone
in a gradually rising bedframe
lifting me high high high
up into the afterworld
for breakfast
with my spiritual ancestors.

Slowly descending like a deflated
balloon back into my wooden
cross-nailed to the bedposts.

Father, forgive them
for they know not
what
they
do.

Fugees

I know.
I don't know
anything about you
asking me for time
to calculate distances,
traveling heart rates beating like drums
beyond the common cold in a septic tank
filled with Sudanese refugees
blistered toes and all
tiptoeing into Kenyan gates.
I know.
I don't know.

Lone In The Stars

It's more comfortable up here
in the stars. My feet don't
ache mashing against
the concrete.

Liars don't lie in jelly pools
or commercial skits trying
to sell me things
I don't need.

Propositions don't pass my
rights away and rights don't
pass me by.

I can be me in the stars—
better than an empty two-bedroom
apartment with walls
and appliances staring me down
to my core

gravity's pushing me more more,
way way up here in the stars.

Nappy Rain

I have nothing left for you,
no more blood to siphon out,
you've taken the best part of me
and left the rest parts of me
and I've got nothing left to give.

You've sucked pleasure from my heart
with a needle so so sharp
took matter from my brain
and spread it jelly on grain.

I've given the finest of my greatest abilities
you've left me nothing but empty
and I owe you my insanity
and insane longevity
and lonely mornings
and frozen midnights.

You've taken everything from me, yet
sit in my face
like a sheet of invisibility

glass a wise shade of blue,
I have nothing left for you.

Coltrane

John is my soul
everything I wish to say
and nothing that I can

nothing that I can

he is several heavy-years
ahead of where I've been
and the places I have
longed to go

John gives me cold fires
and bitter smoke-filled pits
which seep air into lonely
lungs like cigarettes
and ashes.

Purple Sun

The Bobbie Jean Poems:

I Have Always Been Lonely

Since you left me in 1996,
I have always been lonely.

And you have stayed
away from almond-covered
tree trunks growing inside my
brain matter

smudged in fertilized soils
flaking off my skin.

You loved me more yesterday,
straightening my bowtie arrow sharp,
boomerang to sheet wood
spatula to spoon

cooking 8-course dining feasts,
pineapples upside down on cakes.

Complementing my un-sorrowful midnights
unbuttoning my straight-leg Levi's fly
lifting my spine chord
up to the sky.

If You could turn dust to
creatures, she could have stayed
for longer

       instead

I have always been lonely since
you left me.

I Took The Bones Out For You

She didn't like anything hard
in her salmon and rice.

Daddy always made it
such to
teach us the power of tooth
enamel.

"Bobbie,
I took the bones out for you."

Before she flew on up there
with Jesus,
she always told me
I was her
special boy.

Sure wish
I still had that
goldfish from the Salinas
carnival—won in 1993,
when she drove that
midnight black Nissan
crutching her way down
the paved parking lot.

The Calaveras Street Happenstance:
"What Do You Do When A Soldier Goes Home?"—And Other Intricate Questions

I used to see him on Calaveras St.
bumping around in that maze of a garage
barricaded in out-dated refrigerators and
past-due pasty paints—
waiting for Jason, Sam, Bernie, and the
rest of us boys to repaint that worn house border fence.

Red red redness cracking from the center
vortex of an aged backyard picnic bench set
on that summer's 73 degree afternoon I saw
him on Calaveras St.

And he had the   *nerve*!   to have
me repaint that fence

mixing and churning like that tattered
homemade ice cream maker set
which resurfaced every holiday season.

We remember him prancing around
and about with that white Notre Dame
sweater and cap when I used to see him on
Calaveras St.

Making it known that this home
only had room for 49er adorers
and if doubt loomed in our minds,
he was certain to hit the "big time"
with those 7-Eleven dollar scratchers
at Christmastime.

And what do we do when a soldier goes home?

Back from traveling on voyages—
fort to fort to fort to fort to fort
Germany to Switzerland
Korea to Canada
Indiana to California

5 babies gazing up in   to glass
eyes—wondering when the warring
would end.

I couldn't hear enough tales of war—
enough of the medallions
            lain neatly in a tender casing
enough of the difficulties defending a country
            still shackled silly by the unyielding
clench of Jim Crowism
            and illuminated vibrant color lines.

Standing atop a mound of bodies in the
Sub-earthly Vietnam 2:00 PM heat.

But what do we do when a soldier goes home?

Escaping the brutality of disease
broken memories of Korean politics
a famished and worn down soul
from the   weight   of
seeing Black bodies
swinging from poplar trees
then courageously defending America
despite its non-optional racist mentality.

What do we do when a soldier goes home?

To rest with rested heroes
John Jr.—Betty Ann
John Sr.—Izola
Mother—Father
home to simple quietnesses
harmonious wholenesses

peacefulness   like rushing rapids
racing from the belly of mountaintops
to an absolute eternity of ocean waves.

What do we do when the cage
of life has loosened its release valve?

What do we do when the spirit is
emancipated from its fleshly captivity?

What happens after the final
tear drops like plummeting 50 pound boulder
from the eyeball of his baby?

What happens when the African
griot gives libation and calls the name
Willie Cornelius Wells
and the crowd affirms him with
"Ashe   Ashe   Ashe   Ashe-O
        all is well with his soul . . ."

We look to that Notre Dame sporting father,
dollar scratching child of Indiana,
50-year life-partner
who loved to make ice cream at
Wintertime—the man I
used to see on Calaveras St.

and we say "well done soldier
at ease—   at ease"
save a place
for me.

Collard Greens

life's spaceship
lost amid the seas,
drowned in happy sorrows
like Sunday afternoon
collard greens.

My Unfavorite Things

Chit'lins and pumpkins
red peas with no grits,
snow in the winter and
cheddar on Ritz
fruit cake at Christmas and
babies in slings,

these are a few of my
unfavorite things.

Loud screaming kids chasing
flown up balloon strings,
cheese cubes on trays,
dogs neutered and spayed,
rappers with bling and
fat fingers in rings,

these are a few of my
unfavorite things.

When my belly sticks out
when the chins grow
my little black gums
or my yellow bucked teeth
hair falls out gently
or turns squeamish pink

I just remember my
unfavorite things
and then my life
ain't
so
bleak.

Waters Rise Up

these lonesome waters
welling up in my soul

a once vibrant vessel
crafted to be sold

for millions and millions
in an old gallery's room

made of diamonds and
emeralds, copper and pearl

waters rise up inside me
can't breath, can't see

these lonely waters
won't get out of me

Rock Amongst Seashells

Seems like it's harder
to live

like a seasoned star
in-between planet and
asteroid

floating on blood waves like
cinder blocks from
eucalyptus.

Stomach dropped seven times
today, hoping to spoil
yesterday's raindrops.

Who wants to live a rock amongst
the seashells?

Uglified, black, chipped-out,
hard.

A Lonely

Mountains peaking mid-air,
grass blades trapped in
lawn mower bags,
the letter 'Z' in the back
and puppies sold off,
the north star pulling down
southern state breaking odd
single while light switch at night
plastered in several pounds of
darkness—
backlights illuminating empty
jail cells
the last piece of baked
chicken swimming in grease
dirty dishes left to rot
in the sink
wrapped Christmas presents
shoved in hallway closets a single
fish without its ocean,
waves settled in the seas
life vests preserved
tea kettle screams
yesterday's news and old
wedding shoes—left to burn
in the blackness
in the absent.

Handcuff Symphony

tried to be a good kid
prayed every night

that god would take the
pills from my hand

but older and older the
curse prevailed me and
stole my possibilities
one   by   one

mama said—
"you know you weren't
raised like that"

daddy cried—
"no son of mine"

and I sat there
knees bent on heels
praying to be freed
unbroken from these

handcuffs on my mind,
this broken symphony.

Feeling Sorry For Myself

So lonely over here
like that last icicle
hanging on an
empty rain gutter.

Like the sun after the
clouds have spread
lost and alone—
traveling the cyclical
realm of aliveness.

Dirtiness in my tears
beating heart bleeding
red eyeballs.

So lonely over here

on my sorrow's couch
feeling sorry for myself
feeling sorry for myself
feeling sorry for myself
feeling sorry for conscience

feeling the browning of
my loins

feeling the oven on
my gums

feeling the lightning rod pierce
my brain

James B. Golden

feeling the feelings of
someone feeling sorry for himself

feeling sorry for myself
so lonely tonight

so lonely over here

so lonely over here

so lonely over here

so sad

so saddened

so alone

all alone.

I Don't Think I Can Do This

Can't put the knife in my
vein. Stop the blood.

Racing to membranes.
Stop my eyes from filling
each night.

Can't hold the 9MM
shotgun to my guts
blowing insides out of
proportion.

To the backseat of my
325i.

Bullets   Bullets   Bullets
everywhere.

All around me.

Brown Sky Dandruff

Sat up high atop daddy's
shoulders—stretching
arm limbs further
than yesterday flipping
light switches on
and moonlight becomes you.

Boy, oh boy
son   your arms flail
around rapidly smelling every
centimeter of unoccupied
skyscape. Dancing with
baby eagles playing
with the blue
and moonlight becomes you.

Humming daddy's song
to a six-foot plunge
sprinkling brown sky dandruff
on poppies at spring
eyes opened up   up   up
he flew
and moonlight becomes you.

While You Had No Job

I loved you at a time
when you didn't love yourself
lubricated your skin,
kept your veins wet
breathed my essence into
your lifeless body
and you left me out here
to dry like
salt pork.

Someone I Knew Before

Sip of wine,
toasting the night.
Glanced to the right, saw
someone I knew before
straight shot from my eyes
and I died for a while.

Eyes big as boulders
rolling down rivers,
bloody and soiled by
staining memories.

She and him
sitting politely,
eating contritely,
crushing my soul.

I never meant to be alone,
or see another man love the
someone I knew before.

goodbye

I guess this is my goodbye to
you. I tried my hardest to
be a 'good enough' man . . .

I AM A MAN.
I AM A MAN.
I AM A MAN.

Even though you say I'm not.

I hate this life.
I'll send it back,
I swear.

Don't judge my actions
just love my compassion,

the words I've penned
the eraser's all that's left.

goodbye.

Notes

Page 6: "Don't Touch My Hair" first appeared in Kapu-Sens Literary Journal, Fall 2008.

Page 7: The final stanza of "I Rise Up In You" is a reference to *Lift Ev'ry Voice And Sing* by James Weldon Johnson.

Page 15: The title "Our Nig" is a reference to the slave narrative of Harriet E. Wilson. The full title of her 1859 book is *Our Nig: Sketches From The Life Of A Free Black*. It is considered the first book published by an African American in North America.

Page 17: "I Am The Authentic Man (Rap Version)" was written for Grandmaster Flash, DJ Kool Herc, and Jazzy Jeff. It is dedicated to the memory of the coldest of them all, Jam Master Jay. The epigraph is a reference to "God Is A DJ".

Page 20: "Didn't Ask You To Alter My Thoughts (On Vinyl)" first appeared in Kapu-Sens Literary Journal, Fall 2008.

Page 27: The title, "In The Presence Of Mine Enemies", is a reference to Psalms 23:5, one of the most stirring verses.

Page 29: "Letter No. 5 To An Absent Mother" was written for Willie and Kevin. The poem features some of their own powerful language.

Page 51: "Crucify Me" references Luke 23:34 at the end of the poem.

Page 54: Written for my dearest cousin who experienced heartache no one should have to endure at such an early age.

Page 59: "The Bobbie Jean Poems" were written for my dearest auntie, Barbara Jean Benjamin-Hairston, who was my heart and soul.

Page 61: My dad was cooking salmon and rice on our kitchen stove, when he looked up to the sky and said, "Bobbie, I took the bones out for you". I wrote this poem on a kitchen table napkin and stored it away for what seemed like eternity.

Page 62: "The Calaveras Street Happenstance" first appeared at the funeral of my Uncle W.C. Wells, for whom the poem was written. It was also published in Kapu-Sens Literary Journal, Fall 2008.

Page 75: You know who you are.

Page 79: "Brown Sky Dandruff" is for my father. I would climb high up and fall asleep in his arms every single Sunday during our church prayer hour.

Acknowledgements

"Praise the bridge that carried you over."

—*George Colman*

The author wishes to thank all family members and friends who have enriched his life terribly.

Thanks to the parentals—Valerie and James.

To all those who laughed, cried, gasped and covered their mouths while workshopping these poems—thanks.

Finally, all credit is placed in the hands of God, who orchestrated this monster.

Peace & Blessings

About the Author

James B. Golden was born and raised in Salinas, California, and received his M.P.A. and B.A. in English and Pan-African Studies Arts & Literature from California State University, Northridge. He has edited Kapu-Sens Literary Journal and the Hip Hop Think Tank Journal. He is the author of *Sweet Potato Pie Underneath The Sun's Broiler*. He currently lives in Los Angeles, where he is a freelance music journalist. His articles have appeared in such periodicals as Clutch Magazine, Jazz Times, and Our Weekly.

For more information, please visit www.JamesBGolden.com.